TIFFANY DAWN KOHNEN

Can You See Me Now?

To my daughter Sonja.
I can't wait to meet you and experience life with you!

And to all blind and visually impaired people who wish they could educate the public on how other can help the blind—

This is for you.

-Tiffany Kohnen

Other Books in the series Can You Help
Me Now?

Can You See Me Now? (Oct 26, 2015)
Can You Hear Me Now? (June 30, 2021)
Do You Feel Me Now? (Dec 30, 2021)

Social Channels
Facebook.com/DBLadylife
www.KohnenBooks.com
Insta: @Koh.nen

Contents

Foreword

How many times have we seen someone who looks as if they might need a bit of support, but we have held back as to not interfere?

Or continued to walk by even if the person asked for assistance because we did not feel comfortable or did not know how to be of service? Or seen someone who is doing a task slowly or differently and rushed in to "do it for them," then wonder why they were not grateful?

These are all common scenarios a person with a vision loss may encounter every day. The public often have assumptions or questions about blindness, or maybe they have never even given it a second thought.

In this book, Tiffany Kohnen shares her feelings, life examples and suggestions on how to glimpse the world as she sees it and lend support from her perspective of being an independent and active person who has a progressive vision loss that may lead to total blindness.

From the time I met Tiffany in 2007, her vision has changed drastically, and she has made accommodations along the way, never letting it stand in the way of her reaching her goals and setting new ones. She has always walked to her own beat, expressing herself in her own style of clothing, in her art, and in the songs she writes and sings accompanied on her ukulele.

The minute you say the words "blind" or "visually impaired," a whole list of things a person cannot do may come to mind: driving, riding a bicycle, shopping, traveling and sight-seeing, skiing, woodworking, cooking, running a marathon, karate, and the list goes on.

When, in reality, most things CAN be done with supports, adaptations and a "can do" attitude.

Patrick, a young man with very little vision, recently completed a triathlon. He could see the lines in the pool to swim in his lane, but needed a "pilot" to ride tandem for the biking portion of the race and a person running with him connected by a cord on each of their wrists to the run course of the race.

Sometimes, it just takes the will and some ingenuity to work together to devise a method that will work to allow access and participation and, ultimately, a fulfilling life.

Tiffany describes how to provide support, allowing the person with vision loss to take the lead on what and when they want help.

This is a good read for persons who are blind or losing their vision, parents and family members of people with vision loss, professionals in the field of vision, employers and co-workers, community folks, and potential friends.

This book is for anyone who wants a better understanding of typical obstacles people with vision lo's face and how we can lend support, plan to make areas and activities accessible, and how to be creative to work around perceived barriers.

In my work over the past 25 years with people with vision and hearing loss, it is the personal contact and learning from those who are blind or who have "low vision" that has taught me the most on helping people to Dream Big and reach for the stars! Tiffany has written an easy-to-read guide to get you started on a fulfilling adventure!

Emily Taylor-Snell, M. Ed.
    University of Florida
    Florida and Virgin Islands Deaf-Blind Collaborative
    Co-Author and Contributor to NCDB Transition Toolkit

and Open Hands, Open Access Modules

Acknowledgement

I have never finished a book by myself. Writing a book is not a solo craft for writing non-fiction works.

That said, I want to take the time to thank the people who helped me put this book together. First, I want to thank the love of my life, Richie Morales. He passed away a few months ago as of this second publication. He was a steadfast, strong, smart, and honest man. I met no one who faced so many trials in one lifetime and could stand tall on his feet and ready to keep on helping people. I love you, Richie. Thank you for the deep and abiding love, the support you gave, and your belief in me.

Next, I want to thank Emily Taylor-Snell for the input she has given me on this book, and to honor me with writing the Foreword. She is a Deaf-Blind specialist from the University of Florida. She goes out into the communities all over Florida and the United States to help children and young adults who have vision and hearing loss gain access to the world at large. She is both my mentor and my colleague, and I am also proud to call her a friend of mine. Thank you, Emily!

I also want to thank the Healthy Families which sparked me to set personal goals, and my counselor April Jones was the fire-starter to dream big again. It is my desire to write, and to start a company to help inspire people with disabilities to share their stories.

Another supportive friend who contributed some content to this book is Becki Forsell. She was one of the most amazing women I had ever had the pleasure of meeting. With her experience of being legally blind for two decades, she had a lot to add to this book. She also provided many words of wisdom on not just being legally blind or how people with disabilities live fulfilling lives, but on life itself. We are who we are, not our disability. Thank you, Becki, for being a wonderful friend and like a second mother to me.

I also want to thank Melissa Linde-Powers Julie Kramer, and Jennifer Anderson for taking the time to read the book and provide their valuable input and thoughts on the book. Without it, the book would not be ready for publication. Thank you, ladies!

For the cover designer, I want to thank Starla Huchton. She is the designer of the series and I am absolutely in love with her work. If you want something similar for your projects, check her stuff out!

She also is designing for my fiction series, The Hidden Tales. www.designedbystarla.com

I want to thank several Facebook groups who have helped contribute knowledge and words of encouragement to this book. They base one on Retinitis Pigmentosa, and the other a support group for Christian authors. Without these two groups, this book would not have been the same. Thank you, everyone. The three groups in question are:

Room With A View–Visually Impaired Expressive Women
   Retinitis Pigmentosa Support Group (The RP Family Group)
   The Time is Write

I want to thank my dad for being an inspiration. He is a go-getter and determined to get things done. His knowledge of business has helped in the way I plan to start my business. If not for him, my passion to help people would remain dreams with no place to take shape. Thank you, Dad, for showing how to make dreams a reality.

Finally, I thank God for instilling this passion of mine in writing and in helping people learn something meaningful. Without knowing God, I would remain a dreamer. To go from a dreamer to a person with action, one must actually do and not continue to dream. God, thank you so much for the love you have surrounded me with, and for showing me the way to step out in faith.

THE *CAN YOU HELP ME NOW* SERIES

14 EFFECTIVE STRATEGIES TO INTERACT WITH AND HELP THE VISUALLY IMPAIRED AND THE BLIND

CAN YOU SEE ME NOW?

TIFFANY DAWN KOHNEN

FOREWARD BY EMILY TAYLOR-SNELL

Dawn Of Writing Publishing
www.Facebook.com/DawnOfWriting
www.KohnenBooks.com
Kohnen@dawnofwriting.com

0 | Introduction

You see them in the streets, at the mall, or they may even be a friend or family member. Some are not blind as a bat, but nearly so.

Some experience progressive loss of vision leading to blindness, or others' sight remains stable their entire lives, and still others are totally blind. Each of them is legally blind for a wide variety of reasons, including disease, birth, or trauma. Trauma can happen to anyone. Some can lose their eyes in a random act of violence, as it happened to my fiancé, who wore glass eyes.

I have Usher Syndrome, which includes retinitis pigmentosa (RP). RP is a genetic disease of the eye which causes first night blindness, then tunnel vision and finally the loss of central vision. There is no cure for either RP or Usher Syndrome.

Happily, there are some very promising retina chips and gene therapy that are in the testing stages.

Right now, my left eye's vision sees the world like looking through a wavy ocean. I have about 10 degrees of vision compared to a pair of normal eyes having 120 degrees. People whose eyes doctors can correct to 20/20 vision, we call them sighted people. People with corrected vision but still exceed 20/200 or with narrow vision we call legally blind or visually impaired. They should not be driving cars.

With less than 15 degrees of vision, I can see nothing on either side of my face or above and below me. For this reason, I walk into a lot of poles, trip over things left on the floor, etc., and I have scars to prove it. Yet, I rarely felt like I'm blind because I still have central vision, and I can read print just fine. Though reading is easier if I have a bigger font size, or white or yellow text on a black background.

The biggest challenge for me happens when I move from point A to point B. My eyes cannot scan around my surroundings fast enough, making me guess, and never allowing me to be sure there are no obstacles.

Even if I take a moment to scan, will still miss things, even as obvious as a Wet Floor sign or a pole, not to mention cars. I have had some near misses when I'm on the streets.

The purpose of writing this book is to show you there is a shade between the totally blind and the sighted people. How you can avoid social faux pas and help someone who is either fully blind, partially sighted, and even help others who struggle with accepting that they are going blind. How can you reach out to those people with a distinct set of needs?

For the deaf, you know, to speak up louder, for the mobility challenged, you know, to slow down and walk at their pace. So, how about the blind? Do you just grab their hand and show them the way? Actually, no, that's the worst thing you can do.

The differences I've already told you between my fiancé and me illustrates that there are varying degrees of blindness. Some legally blind people need glasses in order to see anything, others need a special TV to read books with a larger magnification, and still others need a cane or a service animal to navigate their world.

Next time you come across someone who has a cane or a service dog, and they look you in the eye, you might think: *'Aren't you blind? Are you faking it to screw us over?*, or you may even straight up ask a blind stranger with the white cane: "Hey you, you obviously can see... You know that cane is for blind people, right?" Or, as a lot of legally blind people often hear: "But you don't look blind."

This book covers fourteen topics and tips on how you can successfully interact with a stranger, a friend, or a loved one who is dealing with vision loss. There is no shame in losing one's sight, only a new adventure to be embarked on.

Being blind is just another way of life. We may not depend on cars, so public transit is a big part of our lives. Yet, even in our world of being blind, we all still share the same human experience as you. You deal with relationship problems, so do those of us with vision loss. You laugh at jokes, we can crack a joke too!

1 | What "Blind" Isn't

Before we delve into how you can interact with the visually impaired and the blind community, there are a few things *not* to do!

Each disability is different and does not co-exist except if the person has multiple disabilities, such as deaf-blind, or a blind person in a wheelchair. Each disability prevents someone from having the ability to do something, such as hear, see, or walk.

If the ears don't work, it does not mean the eyes also do not work and, consequently, don't read Braille. Even Marlee Matlin, the well-known Deaf actress, was given a Braille menu by a flight attendant.

One type of disability also does not always mean the person is mentally challenged, which is another form of disability. Next, in the paragraph following the story of the Doctor completing his residency on the bus.

* * *

You recently received a Ph.D. from Yale and just started your residency with a high-profile doctor in Boston. On your way to the hospital, you wait at the bus stop with your white cane out. Someone approaches the bus stop.

"Oh hello sir, do you need some help?" someone asked you.

"No thanks, I got it," you reply, holding back a sigh. It's often you hear strangers' offer to assist, and today you really did not want to be bothered. You are thinking about the patient you would assist the doctor with today. The patient has a very complicated nerve damage.

"No really, I'll help you get on, it's okay. I'm not a scary stranger," the woman said, sounding like she's talking to a seven-year-old child. You tilt your head, stupefied with your mouth slack jawed.

The bus screeches and stops in front of you, and before you move towards where the door might be, the woman grabs your wrist and starts tugging you forward in another direction.

"Wait, wait, it's this way," she said. You tried to interrupt her and pull away, but the stranger tightens her grip on you.

"It's okay, sir. Don't be scared," she said.

"Excuse me?" you say as you're forcibly pulled onto the bus. "Lady, let me go."

"Aw, it's okay. You're safe now," she said, letting go of you. "Where's your card at? I'll swipe it for you."

"I'll do it, thank you," you said, moving towards the card reader machine with your card ready.

"Aw, you've done this before? What a big boy you are," she said as the card is yanked from your hand just as you were about to swipe it.

Gritting your teeth, you turn to the driver.

"Excuse me, driver, this lady won't leave me alone," you said.

"Ma'am, I've been giving this gentleman his ride to his work every day for a few months now, leave him alone," the driver said and the woman lets out a huff.

"But he needs help!"

"Excuse me, lady, I have a Ph.D., and I'm doing my residency at the hospital, so please back off."

* * *

It is offensive to the person with a disability to be treated like they have a different disability than the one they actually have, most commonly being treated like a mentally challenged person. It is the most humiliating treatment people with disabilities receive, being viewed as an individual with a mental retardation or as someone who is still mentally a child.

It is degrading to someone who has done things for themselves in their lives and to not be recognized as a person with functioning mind.

I encourage you to not treat anyone with a disability as having a mental capacity of a five-year-old child unless you want to be told off by them or be treated rudely by them. I will give you that some people with disabilities will often tolerate you if they want to get on with their day, but in their minds, they will think poorly of you and any chance of forming a friendship with you will most likely be lost.

To conquer the mindset about people with disabilities having mental challenges, try having high expectations of them. Expect they can do more than you think they can do. Don't rush to help someone, but stand to the side and let them know you're there to help if they need it. Get into a discussion with them about life, what's on the news, the weather. Let them take the lead, and you can follow.

Having this mindset will more than likely lead to them in respecting you as an individual. Like you, they have dreams they are reaching for.

If you have low expectations of them, expecting that they are incapable of caring for themselves, then one of two things will happen: Either they will prove you wrong on principal or they will have less incentive to have you think otherwise. Having low expectations can make them feel undervalued.

If they have no incentive to prove you wrong, it can also create a thought pattern of: "If they don't expect me to achieve anything, then why bother? I'll just sit here and let them do it for me. It's easier that way."

Set high expectations of them, and you might just be surprised to see what will happen next.

One last thing I want to bring up here. People with no disability often confuse or combine the needs of those with disabilities. Deaf people are given Braille menus in restaurants or information in Braille in-flight on airplanes. In the same way, many visually impaired and blind people share the experience people speaking louder as though the visually impaired person is deaf instead of being blind.

I understand it might be a reflex or a subconscious thing, but be aware of your interaction with the blind. Remember that their ears are working fine, they just can't see. Do your best to not raise your voice, thinking they need to compensate for their loss of sight by increasing your volume of voice.

However, as you may have heard, senses that were lost will often heighten other available senses. Talk normally, and they will ask you to raise your voice if they have difficulty hearing you.

Vision loss has nothing to do with their mind, their ears, or the rest of their bodies. If in doubt, when you meet people with vision loss, talk to them as though they can see.

2 | The Stigma

We would all like to believe that there are no longer any stigmas attached to people with disabilities (PWD). The reality is the public still shies away from interacting with someone with a disability. It creates a sense of rejection in PWD, even if it was done unintentionally.

For those who know a PWD it's easy to overlook they may still struggle with joining in social activities that are not adapted to their disability. In the following story, imagine you are a dad with vision loss attending your kid's soccer practice.

* * *

You're at your son's first soccer practice, and you're sitting in the bleachers. You hear a gathering of parents nearby, and you want to connect with them. You get up and trip over some seats and stairs, creating a loud ruckus as you go to the gathered parents.

Out of breath, you introduce yourself, "Hello!"

The conversation in the group ceases. They don't ask if you're okay, and you feel your face heat up.

"I'm, ah, Michael."

"Oh… It's…, nice to meet you," a woman said, "I'm Molly… So… You have a son playing here?"

"That's right," you replied with a sense of pride. Before you could ask about their kids or themselves, Molly continues with their previous conversation where they left off.

"And, uh, right, this girl was awful. She would not help me at all in locating the popcorn section in the chips aisle. It simply was not stocked there even though she said it was and…"

You stand there a little awkward for a moment, listening to the conversation, then backed away without saying another word.

* * *

Most of the time, it doesn't happen this overtly. The visually impaired person will usually skip joining the group and simply sit by themselves, wishing someone else would join them for some company. They think, "I'm sitting here, alone. I'd go up to them and join in the conversation, but I don't want to make a fool out of myself while I walk over there, or get shunned. Don't they see me sitting here by myself? Come on, talk to me!"

There are other reasons to stay by themselves that might come into play. They would rather stay in one place so they don't trip over themselves while carrying around a drink. To minimize any potential hazards to themselves and others, they remain stationary the whole time.

However, this usually means they are off to the side and are by themselves. They watch and hear the going-on, but only from the outside. To them, it's like looking through a window of a closed store at the shopping mall, desiring to buy, yet unable to go into the store and get it.

After the gathering, parties and other social activities, they usually end up feeling miserable and isolated. Yet, even if you asked them if they enjoyed themselves, they will usually say they had a good time. They don't want you to feel bad for them, so they lie with a smile.

You'd usually never know, because you were not paying attention to others, people who are sitting by themselves. It's understandable and not your fault if you're in the middle of the festivities and focused on the people immediately surrounding you. It's easy for other details of the party to fade from your mind. It happens. With that in mind, I have a challenge for you.

Next time you are at a gathering, put your observation skills to the test. If you see someone with vision loss or another forms of disability, and they attempted to interact with people where you are, and later, you see them sitting by themselves. Get yourself, and maybe one other person, over to the person, then start chatting up.

The reason I suggest bringing a second person along is to maintain the spirit of company, and they won't feel as singled out as they would if it's done one-on-one.

If you take this action, it's quite possible the one thing they will remember most from the gathering is their discussion with you, and enjoying your good company.

Another suggestion in becoming more inclusive of people with vision loss or other forms of disability is to consider inviting another person with a similar disability.

It would give each of them a chance to make new friends who have the same condition as themselves. The more you can invite, the better.

I want to caution you, do not make it appear like a set-up play date so they would 'babysit' each other and not be a part of the actual group.

To avoid this type of situation, it's suggested that people with vision loss are not by themselves in a silo but to intermingle with the rest of the group. Other people without a disability could even learn a thing or two about vision loss when the discussion of being legally blind comes up.

The more inclusive gatherings become, the better experience everyone will have. People will gain new perspectives on life, a different spin on many topics such as how driverless cars might affect the

Blind community, and even creative new ideas and solutions to problems no one else has thought of may be pointed out. The experience becomes more enriching and worthwhile for all. It is my hope the stigma of interacting with PWD will fade.

3 | Talk About It

The person you know or meet may not be the first person you have come across who is visually impaired because a lot of the times you won't even know they're legally blind.

The visually impaired can be pretty good at hiding their disability. There are many people who have low vision, yet function like a sighted-person. Some still even drive cars.

For some, they don't want you to know they are legally blind because they refuse to accept they have low vision issues, or rather, don't want others to look at them differently.

No matter the reason, it will be up to them to either tell you themselves or display it with an action that is very blind-centric; for example, they may carry a white cane.

* * *

My friend Becki had this happen to her the other day. She was at a function talking to a woman at a table. Once they were done talking, Becki got up from the table, and she unfolded her white cane.

The woman Becki was talking to was so startled, she blurted out, "I didn't know you were blind."

"Well, did you see me as Becki when we were talking?" my friend asked.

"Yes…"

"Do you still see me as Becki now that you know I'm blind?"

"Yes…"

"Well, there we have it. Disability doesn't define me, I am my own person."

* * *

Some visually impaired people are often afraid of what people will do or that they will think of them differently. They're not wrong to have such doubts about the sighted people. There is still a lot of resistance against people who are legally blind.

There was a recent headline news article from Norway in July 2015 about a McDonald's restaurant forcing a blind woman to leave the establishment in tears in front of her 5-year-old daughter. The reason she was forced to leave was because the woman had a guide dog assisting her. The mom was mortified.

Not only that, consider these statistics in the U.S.: Just 40% of all working-age adults who are visually impaired or blind hold at least part-time jobs.[1]

Few work and can't live independently. The facts are in front of us—many in the general population believe people with vision loss are unemployable. Whether it is the costs associated with employing them, liability, or simply think the visually impaired don't have the skills necessary to do the job effectively. It affects employers' hiring decision, even though discrimination is against the law.

One of the ways to tackle this is to talk about vision loss. We need to have an open and honest discussion about what it means to them to be legally blind, how it affects their ability to do different tasks and what they do to accommodate themselves and get things done. You may find many people who are legally blind will be happy to talk and educate you, and let you know what sort of things they can do despite their inability to see like you can.

Fear of the unknown is no longer an excuse when there is a plethora of information available to the public. There are groups of people who are ready to educate others on how they live their lives, if only the public took the time to learn about them! By simply reading this book, you have already taken that step, and I thank you for taking the time to learn.

Now, you may ask: how can even a complete stranger broach the subject of discussing a disability with someone they see on the streets?

Or in a job interview?

My suggestion to you is, have a mindset of a willing student ready to learn.

One day, you might sit down in the bus or a train, and you might see someone across from you who has an obvious disability. Let your curiosity take over. However, before straight up asking you want an answer to, some suggested ways to start a discussion with the person could be:

"Excuse me, do you mind if I ask you some questions? I want to learn more about the experiences of other people with disabilities."

This shows you have respect for the privacy of the other person and want to start a conversation with them. Depending on their answer, you can ask your questions. If they rather not, drop the subject and go back to whatever you were doing. Don't take it personally if they say no.

One reason could be because they know they're getting off soon and don't want to start a potentially long discussion that will suddenly be ended at their stop.

Or it may be just shyness and just not wanting to talk to strangers just now. Whatever the reason, it's probably not you, so don't take it personally. But if they say yes, go for it!

4 | Identify Yourself

On a Sunday morning at a religious function, I was in in a crowded dark place. My fellow church-goers' faces were shrouded in the shadows. Suddenly, I was greeted by someone inside my personal space.

"Hi Tiffany!"

I looked at the person, trying to recognize her face as I gave her a hug. I'm wondering who the woman I'm hugging. I'm pretty sure I know this person, but is it the pastor's wife or my close friend?

Taking a chance, I said, "Hey Margie!"

"Ah, no," she said. My heart dropped.

It turns out it's my close friend and not the pastor's wife who continued speaking into my ear, "It's me, Mary-Anne."

* * *

This a true story that happened to me a few years ago. These types of situations happen more the worse someone's vision gets. The faces people knew become unrecognizable and look like someone else they know.

To avoid the embarrassment or ask who you are, some of them

will stare at you for a few moments trying to figure out who you are. The moment becomes awkward when the blind person says nothing. Eventually the two of you will talk, and the blind person will try to gather clues about you to the list of who they know.

As the conversation topic turns to something that helps give clues to who you are, an ah-ha moment happens. If you recognize some clues that they don't recognize you, you can help them speed up that awkward moment by sharing something about yourself that only the two of you would know, such as what movie the two of you recently saw. Or you can simply say your name.

They don't want to embarrass themselves by making you think they forgot you. If you are a stranger, a simple introduction works because they could wonder if they know you and might pretend to act like they already know you.

When a visually impaired person mistakes you for someone else, just say something like: "Ah, this is Mary-Anne." Don't make a joke out of it unless you know them well and know they won't be offended by it.

When these instances happen more often, they may become more confident to ask you to identify yourself. You will then know you need to announce yourself whenever you come up to them. When they ask, simply and quickly answer the question and don't continue to make it embarrassing for them.

5 | Talking To Themselves

"…and then I fell down, smacked my face and that's how I chipped this tooth," your friend said, showing you that his front tooth is half gone. "So, I must go see the dentist soon. I'm glad it's not hurting right now."

"I hope it won't be too expensive!" you said. "I feel you, bro, I chip my teeth all the time, it seems. Not fun being blind as a bat."

"I'll say," he replies. "If only that patch of ice had salt. I should sue them…"

"Hahaha, yeah, you should," you said as the room grows darker with the sun setting. "So, when will you go get that fixed?"

Silence.

"Carl?" you ask, looking around, straining your eyes to see where your friend is. "Carl?" After a few moments, you see Carl is nowhere in sight.

* * *

Nothing annoys a blind person more than discovering they were talking to themselves for several moments and discovering the person they thought they were talking with had vanished. It is one of the most common pet peeves people in the blind community share. It makes them feel foolish and wondering if anyone has seen them "talking to themselves."

The sighted person needs to be aware of their interaction with people who are legally blind. The legally blind don't always hear when the person they are conversing with leaves, despite the common fallacy that people who are blind have some kind of magical sound-based radar. Even if the conversation came to a natural conclusion, and you want to do something else, like move to another gathering of people or to use the bathroom, don't simply leave without saying you are going.

The best advice I can give you is to use the same phrases you would use when on the phone. You would not suddenly hang up the phone after a discussion, would you? So, say goodbye or let them know to hang on for a second. The following scenario is the correct way to handle it.

* * *

"Can you believe it? That guy was brainless, cutting me off while I was trying to cross the parking lot," you tell your friend Mandy.

"You could have gotten run over," she said, shaking her head. The room dims in the living room as a movie played on the television.

"I should have given him a re-education on his driving skills," you muttered.

"Yeah... Hey, I need to use the bathroom, I'll be right back," Mandy said. You nod, and she leaves the room at a hurried pace.

6 | Do You Want to Help? You Can Ask!

How do you go about offering your help to the visually impaired and the blind? Ask. It's a simple act, but one that allows the other party to accept or refuse help. When they accept your help, ask them how you can help.

If they don't want to accept help, don't take it personally—they have their own reasons for doing something themselves. That can be anything from maintaining their own independence to not wanting contact with a stranger.

In chapter one, *What Blindness Is Not!*, we saw the example of a gentleman holding a Ph.D. was accosted by a woman who forced her help on him. This is a common example of how someone might go over to a blind person and push their assistance on them without asking.

This is forgiven only in extreme cases, such as if they are about to get electrocuted by stepping on a stray power line on the ground. If, however, their life is not in an immediate danger, you can explain to them, "Hold on! You're about to get hurt!"

Once they stop moving into a potentially dangerous situation, explain why you stopped them. If they don't listen or hear you, they will thank you later after you gently or forcibly pull them away from the danger by their shoulder or arm.

Try not to grab them in a bear hug or any other form of contact that restricts their movement unless absolutely necessary. Trust them to stop when they feel someone touching them because they almost certainly will. Keep in mind that some, if they feel threatened, might hurt you instead by performing self-defense.

If they refuse your assistance, respect their wishes. Some visually impaired people like to maintain their independence wherever they can. They often know their limits, and will accept or ask for help if they know they can't do something themselves.

Those who are losing their vision may often reject your help because they either don't 'feel blind enough' to have help or refuse to accept the fact they are legally blind. Let them try to do a task themselves.

They may want to see if they can do it, and even failing at it is a learning experience. If they consistently fail and accept their inability as fact, they will accept your help more readily the next time. When they are losing their vision, they don't know what the limits are when it comes to performing tasks until they try it for themselves. By allowing them their freedom to do something, they get to learn those changing limits.

The key here for you is to have patience. They want to know what their current limits are, and if they keep getting help with something they can do themselves, they will feel like they are being treated like misunderstood children, and it can lead to resentment against you.

As something becomes more difficult for them, they also may learn to adapt the task. Whatever form of adaptation they take allows them to have the opportunity to learn to speak up and ask for help.

7 | Contrast and Colors

You enter a dark room, lit only by low light lamps on each table, providing just enough light to show where the white chairs are. Everything else blends into one color, deep red. The tablecloth and napkins are dark red, the plates are dark brown; the glasses are clear.

You are seated and ready to peruse the menu. The lettering is barely a different color than the light brown paper. You take your phone out and turn the flashlight app on, blinding the other patrons, including your date.

Once the orders are made, you chat with your blind date.

"So, what do you do?" you ask while you wait for glasses to be filled with wine. You chose red, so you don't appear weird to your date. Yet, you forgot your earlier faux pas—you probably already weirded your date out by blinding her with your flashlight on your phone.

You estimate where the glass is and reach for it, but your hand knocked over the cup of water instead, spraying all over your date.

* * *

A person with vision loss often struggles with colors that are close to one another, and most dark or light colors get mistaken for black or white unless it is put in direct sunlight. The contrast is worse when the lighting is poor because the colors will run into each other.

When you are creating or setting something up for the visually impaired, ask yourself one question: Is there enough contrast?

If in doubt, it's okay to ask the person what works for them. Do they prefer white on black or black on white? Yellow on black or yellow on blue? Is the font thick or small or big?

On that note about large fonts—there *is* such a thing as having too big a font. Don't assume that a visually impaired person needs a huge font size just because they're low vision. For some, a larger font can overwhelm their eyes. Reading is more difficult when they see only one letter at a time, not as a whole word. Some prefer the font smaller so they can increase readability.

Another area to consider about improving their ability to see is lighting. Ask them some questions to find what lighting is best for them. Some experience a lot of glare, so set the room to be a little darker; but others have night-blindness, so grab a lamp or two to brighten up the place. They will let you know what works for them. If they are not sure, you can experiment together!

They may also answer, "Oh, don't worry about it, I'll use my phone to help my way." The smartphone or tablet is an amazing tool for the legally blind because there are many accessibility apps to help enhance their lives, such as identifying colors, magnification, and, of course, turning on the flashlight.

* * *

You are sitting down at the table, and everything is either white or clear.

The server comes to your table to take your orders.

"Excuse me sir, do you have some colored napkins? I can't see where things are on this table."

"Oh, of course. We have a variety of choices, not just place mats but cups and plates too. Do you prefer the red or blue?"

"Red would be great, thank you, except the plate can stay white," you reply, and then everyone makes their orders and then the server leaves.

Several moments later, he returns with several items: a red place mat, napkin, and a red cup. He sets it up for you.

"Is this better?" he asked.

"Much, wish there was more light in here though."

"I can supply another lamp if that will be agreeable?"

You nod your head, and moments later, there are now two lamps lit on the table. You now can enjoy your dining experience for the rest of the night.

8 | Disorientation

For some visually impaired people who can still see, and for others who are totally blind, they often experience disorientation on a daily basis. They will do their best to stay orientated at all times.

This skill of orientation is so important it's a part of the skill training is given to legally blind people: Orientation & Mobility. These instructors are often called O&M Teacher or Instructor. They help and teach new skills to the visually impaired and the blind, such as cane skills, learning where things are in their community, etc.

However, these skills are not foolproof. There will still be instances where the legally blind need to take a moment and figure out where they are. They may ask you to tell them what or which way they are facing. When these questions come up, answer promptly.

When you're out on the street or in a store, and you notice someone is stumbling into things. Don't immediately assume they are drunk or high on drugs. I once got called out as a drunk in Dominican Republic after stumbling up a curb, and it was two in the afternoon.

While I don't expect people of different cultures may not have as much awareness of PWD as the United States or United Kingdom does, it still illustrates what people will think when witnessing someone walking into things.

It happened to another visually impaired woman too during her class reunion, as blogged by Amy Bovaird. She shared how it was nighttime and needed to use a port-a-potty. On the way, she stumbled into bushes and her former classmates saw the whole thing. They thought her a drunk and pitied her.

The visually impaired won't always have a cane with them because they have enough vision to get around in a familiar or well-lit places. It often happens when an object is in their blind spot that don't see and will stumble over it.

If they hit their heads on a pole, ask them if they're OK and need some help, like an ice pack. If they accept your help, help with whatever they ask of you, within your means to accommodate them.

If they are having difficulty navigating and you offered to help, they might say, "I'm alright, just give me a moment," then give them a moment to collect themselves. Their eyes might readjust and establishing things in their minds to orientate themselves.

If you are with a legally blind person and they raise their hand out, ask if they want to grab your elbow so you can guide them to where they need to go. More on this in the *Guiding* chapter on the best practices for guiding the visually impaired and the blind.

Be patient when they need a moment to orientate themselves. Once they are, then you can continue with what you were doing, such as entering the grocery store.

9 | Look Around More!

A hand knocked a coffee mug to the ground, breaking it into dozens of shards. A head banged into a pole and got a concussion. A hand gets cut by a glass while picking up a pen off the ground. It is a fact of life for many visually impaired people, not just the ones who are totally blind, will get injured regularly, and sighted people lecture them, saying:

You need to look around more.
  Be more careful.
  It's right there, can't you see it.

There is one thing that the visually impaired person, especially for those who are experiencing a loss of vision that gets worse over time and is adjusting to their new loss of vision, is they know of their shortcomings. Being told to look around more adds to the stress of the situation than it needs to be. They are already trying to be careful, trying to tell their bodies to slow down, to simply *see* more with what vision they have left.

To help the visually impaired, move past the incident by not making a big deal out of their accidents. Help them through it, and then move on.

Usually, and especially someone with a recent onset of blindness, their body and mind are still operating as though they're not blind, that there's nothing wrong with their eyes. In my experience, bodies are slow to adjust when vision change from bad to worse. It is like the story of the frog and the boiling water in the pot. If you lose eyesight suddenly, adapt quickly.

But, if you are slowly losing vision over a long period, then you remain comfortable where you are at, doing the same thing as before. Before you know it, you wake up one day and try to do the same thing, and the body doesn't know how to cope and still try to do the same thing as before.

A person going blind may put a cup of water down on the table, then later knock it over when reaching for the salt shaker. If something is out of sight, it is out of mind. They forgot the cup of water and did not see it while getting the salt, and then boom, the glass of water is knocked over.

When you say something like:

Be more careful.
   Didn't you see that?
   You need to look around more.
   Slow down.

These statements only cruelly remind them they have vision loss while they are trying to get their bodies to adjust. Visually impaired people who grew up with excellent vision have developed habits like a sighted person.

Unlearning these habits is hard when their eyes convince their mind that they can still operate as they did before when they had better sight. They are not 'blind' yet. Mentally, they are aware they are going blind. It is a war between psychologically knowing and physiologically knowing that you are legally blind.

Yes, being told to be careful is a good attempt to help them adjust quickly. However, being told to "look around more" can add anxiety and self-doubts to the visually impaired person. It will be far more helpful to help them move on and not make a big deal out of it, like screaming at them in frustration.

Humans learn from their mistakes. Let them learn it on their own terms, without outside input or reminders. When their bodies realize they are constantly breaking things or tripping, the body will learn the proper way to avoid these mishaps in their own time.

You can still help them out by offering support. Depending on the person you know or interact with—take their situation and character into account. You can do a few things like:

Laugh it off and say it is normal.

Are you having a bad eye day?

Can I get that for you? - applies to picking something up or cleaning up.

The pen you dropped is by your left foot.

Can/May I help you?

Again, when someone lectures the visually impaired to "look around more," it is not at all productive. Even if they looked around more, they would still miss things. There is a reason they're going blind and trying to find or see obstacles give them a headache. There is only so much they can do to look around more. Patience and understanding are key to their situation.

10 | Strategic Patience

Having patience is so important that it gets its own chapter. As discussed in the last chapter, don't get frustrated when the person who is going blind is messing things up or breaking your grandma's favorite coffee cup.

Instead of reacting in anger, take a deep breath. Take a step back and don't say a word for a few seconds to recollect. In the meantime, the visually impaired person will probably feel horrible, apologizing as they try to clean up the mess, or simply standing there doing the same thing you are, trying to stay calm.

Then you can focus on helping with cleaning up the mess or putting something back into order. After the task is done, you can speak your feelings. Before speaking, make sure you can talk calmly and still speak your mind. It can go something like this:

"Please don't move my jar of sugar? My mom goes nuts if it's moved out of its place," or "That broken cup… it was my grandma's coffee mug… I'm pretty upset about it."

Don't dismiss, hide, or play down your feelings. Share them with the person who either broke it or does something you don't like. Just because they are visually impaired and broke something does not mean you can dismiss your feelings by justifying with telling yourself: "It's just material things. It's nothing. It wasn't his fault. He's blind."

Acknowledge your feelings and let them know, otherwise your resentment and bitterness could grow. Things never end well when someone you love' holds on to resentment. The more this happens, the more resentment can build, and we don't want that.

Yes, it is usually not their fault because they *are* legally blind, however, set a time aside to discuss strategies to prevent the issue from happening again.

All well-adjusted adults, no matter if they have a disability or not, can adopt strategies to minimize risks and damage to persons or property. If we don't take the time to take a step back and address the problem, it can cause issues in your relationship with each other.

Look at the situation you are in or experienced and think of some solutions both of you can adopt to prevent it happening again.

If you cannot think of something, ask the visually impaired person if they have some ideas. Chances are, they might, especially if they have been coached or trained by professionals who work with the blind.

These organizations like the Lighthouse for the Blind often help blind and visually impaired people gain skills to be self-sufficient for life. This conversation can go something like the following scene.

* * *

Cruuush

The glass cup shattered into several dozen shards. Samantha, who is a sighted person, bit her bottom lip to hold back from screaming at her friend. She took a deep breath and let it out slowly. She sees her blind friend about to kneel to pick up the mess.

"No, I'll get it," Samantha said, kneeling on the ground and starts picking up the large shards.

"I can replace it, I'm sorry," Zoe said, standing where she is while Samantha cleaned up the mess of glass shards. Samantha took another deep breath, held it for a couple moments, then got to her feet as she exhaled, carrying the shards in her hands.

"You know, you broke my grandma's special cup, Zoe," Samantha said, dumping the shards of the shards into the trash.

"Oh… oh, no," Zoe said, her face reddening. "I am so sorry!"

"I forgive you," Samantha said, returning to the mess to pick up other shards. "What can you do so this won't happen again?"

"I-I guess I'll try to slow down when getting the punch," Zoe replied.

11 | Use Locator Words

"It's over there."

"Just a little bit further… no, no, the other way!"

"It's right here."

"Just a little further, now…"

"You went too far."

Vague phrases will not help the visually impaired and the blind. I know it's hard to get used to using locator words, but with use, you'll get better at it. Even I struggle with it when I tell my fiancé where things are. I even mix up left and right! So, attempting to use words is better than sticking with vague phrases. The following list are examples of locator words.

Locator Words:

Right

Left

Behind

Front

Inches

Feet

Use these words to set up a sentence when describing where another person or object is in relation to the blind person: "It's five feet to your right," or "A foot behind you."

The more specific you can get with your description, the better. Don't get frustrated or flustered when there is a communication break down between your mouth and your brain. When you're telling the person where something is, have patience with both yourself and them.

It's okay to get the words mixed up, such as right or left. Even the blind can get them mixed up. If you say left, they might go right and smack themselves into a pole. Again, this is where patience with yourself and the visually impaired comes in.

* * *

A visually impaired man misplaced his phone. He heard you enter the room, and he turns towards you.

"Excuse me, can you please tell me where something is? I can't find my phone." he asked.

"Sure," you reply while scanning the area where the man is standing. You spot the white phone on the counter-top close by the fridge. "Is it a white smart-phone?"

"Yeah it is, you see it?"

"Yeah man, it's three feet to the left of the fridge on the counter," you answer, pointing with your finger where it is. The man searched for the phone until his hand touches it.

"Ah-ha!" he said, picking up his phone, turns the screen on. You heard a voice announcing the lock screen on the phone.

"That's it, thanks. What's your name?" he asked you, turning the screen off the phone and pocketing it.

"Glad to help, I'm Jordan."

* * *

This type of situation gives the visually impaired person control over their environment. They may prefer to find the things they misplaced themselves rather than have someone get it for them. Or they may simply ask you to please find their phone and give it to them.

It all depends on the preference of the person you know or meet. Empower them by abiding by their wishes so they remain in control and not being mollycoddled at every corner.

You also notice that Jordan pointed with his finger at the phone to the man who may or may not see the hand gesture. It's perfectly fine to point, it helps you make the connection between your body and your mind.

It will also help someone who may have some residual vision left, and even if they don't, that's okay too. You're used to responding with gestures, keep acting as though they can still see. If you act flustered, it will affect your speech, and the man will pick up on it and wonder why you are flustered, and ask you what's wrong.

Play it cool, do your best to use the right locator words, and be patient with yourself and the legally blind person. Once you have a system in place that works best for both of you in directing the blind where to go, it will be smooth sailing!

12 | Guiding by the Arm

Guiding a going blind person down a path can be a challenge for both parties because the person who can't see well has to learn how to trust the person guiding them, and the person guiding is often inexperienced and may not know how to best guide the visually impaired person. The partially blind person may also refuse help when going somewhere because they feel they can see well enough to get by.

There actually are standards and procedures in how a sighted person can guide the blind. The standards enabled the blind to maintain control over the situation.

One method in guiding the blind is to always lead ahead of the blind. Don't walk backwards in front of them or try to put them in front of you. Leading ahead is the most natural way for anyone to follow, even of it's a sighted person who may need to follow someone else more knowledgeable about where they are than themselves.

Emily Taylor-Snell wrote, describing how you can lead, A "blind person will take the sighted person by the elbow, lining up their arm with their shoulder to be behind the guide's shoulder. Now the pair creates about 1.5 person wide. By keeping the elbow tucked close to the body, the blind person can fell the sighted person's body movements to know which way to walk."

Imagine for a moment you are the one blind and you need to navigate a path filled with unknown obstacles.

* * *

"Hey, wait, wait!" a woman shouts, grabbing your wrists with both of her hands. "Let me help you."

She tugs you through the path with only her hands on your wrist and you have nothing else to balance on. You feel your body is in danger of falling over to the ground because of the way she is pulling on you.

"Hey," you try to say, pulling your hand away, but she has you in a vice grip.

"No, it's dangerous, just come this way."

The direction she is pulling your wrist seems to go in the opposite direction the woman is walking, confusing you. You feel helpless, relying on the help of a complete stranger who refused to let go of your hand and you are apparently on a dangerous path so you can't simply break off and go off on your own.

* * *

This scenario is something a lot of blind and visually impaired people experience regularly. Communication is key when you are guiding someone whose vision is impaired. The woman also failed to describe the surroundings and why the blind person might be in danger.

As you guide the blind and visually impaired, give them description of their surrounding. When I go shopping with my fiancé, I describe the things I see as I go down an aisle. He said no one else does that, and this limited his shopping choices. By telling him what's on the shelves, he could be inspired to try something, or buy something he hasn't had in a while.

When you are approaching a visually impaired person, ask them if they need help to get somewhere. If they say yes, offer them your arm and they will automatically place their hand on your elbow or your shoulder, two places that place them behind you and it offers them stability and sense of direction, including going up or down steps.

If the blind person refuses your help, you can take the moment to explain their surroundings. For example, you are in a road construction area and there are a lot of obstacles the visually impaired person may have not seen. Let them know. Then they can decide to accept your help. If there is no real safe path, offer to walk with them to make sure they're okay. If they still refuse your help, respect their wishes and let them go. It is their decision.

After this, I would reinforce your directive to never put the blind person in front of you. This is especially true when both of you are in an unfamiliar dark place. You also will want to stay calm because if you are tense and worried about the other person's safety. When this happens, blind person will pick up on it and question you.

If the way you walk is not natural, it conveys to the other that you are unsure, and it can cause them to lose trust in you. Walk at your regular pace, and the blind will follow.

The following situation happened to me one time in a small town in Texas. My mom and I needed to go to the restroom, and we found a place to use the facilities. It was a museum for Pearl Harbor during World War II, and it was quite dark.

My mom got behind me and forcefully guided, pushing me in front of her, the pathway to the bathroom was a confusing maze with a lot of twist and turns, and she herself did not know where to go and I did not trust her because she was confused. I felt like in a horror flick, and that she was using me as a shield against some horrible unseen entity that was going to attack us.

Case in point, don't make them go in front of you, even if you're in a familiar place. They will still feel like they are walking into the unknown. Lead the blind, not follow the blind. Here's a list of do's and don'ts when guiding a blind or visually impaired person.

What not to do:
Run up to them without warning and grab them unless their lives are in an immediate danger

Leave them standing in the middle of the room if you need to leave the blind person behind

Not communicating why they might be in danger to the visually impaired person

Hold on to them in a vise grip

Holding them instead of them holding you

Guiding from behind them

Walking backwards, either yourself or the visually impaired

Sticking your arm out from your side if they are holding on to your elbow

What to do:
Explain and describe the surroundings to them

Offer help and respect their wishes if refused

Offer your arm or shoulder to them

Keep your elbow to your sides and let your arm relax when leading them by the elbow

Lead ahead of them first

Give the blind person something to hold on to if you need to step away for a moment, whether it is a table, a pole, etc., so they can feel on solid ground.

When in a crowded or narrow place, put your arm behind your back and the visually impaired person will hold on to your forearm

When guiding a small child who is blind or visually impaired, let them take your wrist

Communicate with them if any special instructions are necessary such as:

"Two steps up/down."

"Get behind me because there's a biker coming."

"Watch your step, there's a lot of cords on the ground."

13 | Service Animals

Service animals are great partners, they now help people with many disabilities. The service animals we are familiar with and that we will cover here are guide dogs helping the blind. Guide dogs exist to serve one purpose: Navigate from point A to point B safely.

The dogs help the blind maintain independence they otherwise would not have. When you interact with a blind person who has a guide dog, keep in mind the following story that illustrate issues that really annoy the Blind Community.

* * *

Grocery bags in one hand, you are leaving the grocery store with your guide dog Vincent leading the way out. Someone bumps into you with their cart.

"Oh, I'm sorry! Are you okay?" a woman asked.

"Yeah, just a light bump, no worries," you reply as you keep walking.

"Oh, that's an adorable dog!" she said, moving to Vincent and begins to stroke on his head. "What a soft fur he has. Do you bathe him weekly?"

"Ma'am, please don't touch the dog. It distracts him, he's a working dog," you said while Vincent is wagging his tail as he moves closer to the woman. You pull him hard away from the woman with Vincent's lead, cutting off her stroking Vincent.

"You're hurting him!"

"No, I'm not. It's how I discipline him to start working again. It's for both his and my safety. If you hadn't distracted him, he wouldn't have to be corrected. If he remained distracted, he won't get us home safely."

* * *

The moral of the story? It is against the rules to pet a guide dog. The reason is because the dog needs to know they are working, and to safely get their human partner from point A to point B. If the dog is new to guiding, it is all the more important that they are not disturbed by anyone except their human partners for the first six months while they are bonding and learning to trust each other.

Before the human and the dog are matched, the blind person will have already mastered the O&M skills to navigate their surroundings with a cane. When they partner up, the guide dog schools will train the human partner new mobility skills and learning to trust their furry partner who will act as their eyes.

When there is no trust between the dog and the blind person, then their safety is in jeopardy. If the blind person can't trust the dog to remain free from distraction, then the dog can't trust the human to decide where to go.

There is another point to consider when you come into contact with service animals in restaurants: feeding them. The service animals are on a strict diet. Any human food fed to them will hurt them.

It can lead to all kinds of health issues, and it can put the dog out of commission for a period of time, whether it's for a few hours to weeks. If the service animal is not working, their partner would be without their furry partner, putting their life at risk.

So, it is important to not give any attention to the service animal or to attempt to give them human food. Doing so will do more harm than good, despite your good intentions. We know they are super heroes because they help people with vision impairment, with epilepsy, PTSD, and other forms of disabilities.

However, at the end of the day, their safety is paramount and is more important than your good intentions of wanting to reward or give attention to the service animal.

The Blind Community does appreciate your attempt at kindness, however misguided, but the kindest thing you can do for them is to ignore the service animal as though they are invisible to you. The human partner constantly rewards the dog and loves them to death, so, do not worry that the dog is not getting enough love! They are getting a lot of it every day.

14 | Use of Cane

Not all visually impaired people will use a cane to assist them with mobility, and some who still have a good amount of vision left will use them to locate hazards their vision might not detect as well as to alert other people in public to their vision impairment.

Whether they use a cane or not, respect their wishes. If the visually impaired are using a cane, and they look at them in the eye, the sighted person will often be confused, and it can become socially awkward for the VI person when the stranger is confused, suspicious or questioning.

For some, their vision is like standing at the beginning of the tunnel and staring out the other end of the tunnel. You can hear the water rushing near the exit's tunnel, but you cannot see where it is. This is true for those who have RP and other vision loss that causes blind spots in their field of vision. Some use their cane to prevent them from walking into a pole or other low-lying obstacles like a trashcan.

Other visually impaired people may not use a cane at all, and they have their own reasons for not carrying one. Perhaps they know they can still navigate their environment safely or are extremely familiar with the layout of their work, store, or their home.

The reason not to use a cane could also simply not having confidence or hold self-doubts about themselves and the world. Some may refuse to accept they are going blind. Others may not be used to using a cane and feel awkward with one.

Sometimes, even I don't use a cane. I am self-conscious of the sound the cane makes, of other people and what they think. When I look at them in the eye, and I have the cane, they might be confused or suspicious, and I don't like to cause confusion or have them suspect me of lying.

I personally have not been accused of faking it, but I have heard from other visually impaired people that some strangers have accused them of faking it.

Even their own ex-husband or wife.

I did have one stranger at a bus transfer station ask me, "Aren't those canes for blind people?"

"Yeah, I can't see very well like you. Without it, I'd walk into things. These canes aren't just for totally blind people," I replied.

I also learned to be careful explaining why I have the cane when men ask me these questions. You never know if they will take advantage of your weaknesses when they learn the extent of your vision loss.

I had a weird encounter with one man at another bus stop that raised a lot of red flags. He said he followed me from the adjacent corner of the intersection. He had crossed two streets to get to me, and he did not intend to ride the bus. He admitted to following me from the gas station because I was wearing a cute outfit.

I don't mean to presume or exaggerate, but he may have been a pimp. I was just glad the bus was only a few minutes away.

He was asking how much I could really see, if I could recognize his face. Yes, I did, I could tell he was brown, of Arabic descent. He was also asking where I worked and where I lived, my age, and other personal questions. I gave him only vague answers. Then the bus came, and I eagerly got on. I never saw him again.

On a related note about him being a potential pimp, it is reported about 30% of all trafficked human beings in Florida have some form of a disability.[2] So, having a cane out can expose and announce that the person is a vulnerable target.

Which had given me more of a reason to play down my disability especially since people don't associate beautiful people with disability—yes, I recognize I possess physical attributes that gives me beauty. What this means, if I put the cane away or 'ignore' people who call out to me, I would either put myself in harm's way because I didn't have out the cane or appear rude to other strangers.

So, how can you help those who are losing their vision adjust to the idea of using a cane as a tool? Let them practice using the cane, ask them why they don't use the cane. Have a discussion and help build confidence in themselves. When you are with them, and they have their cane out, don't announce the obstacles to them, like the curb or stairs. There is a reason why they are using it, so you don't have to tell them the obstacles. They would rather have their cane find things.

I will reiterate: If they have their cane out, don't warn them of hazards, let them find it themselves. They need the practice and to build confidence in their mobility skills and maintain Independence. Saying something while their cane is out is moot and it will annoy the legally blind people. If they get warned constantly, what's the point of having a cane?

To summarize, don't doubt their reason for using or not using the cane. You can have a discussion with them to build confidence in gaining experience with their cane, and let them find the hazards and obstacles with their cane.

15 | Taking It From Here

Wherever and whenever you are out there in the world, there are people with a cane, a guide dog, or stumbling into things in daylight. These people may need you, or they may not. Whatever you are doing with your loved one who is legally blind, have patience, it will help both yourself and your loved one.

When it comes to helping and interacting with visually impaired and blind people, patience is the biggest virtue to have. With patience comes understanding, and understanding will bring order and peace to any situation you may end up in in life. When you take the time to help, you understand and learn what will make things difficult or easier for someone with vision loss.

You begin to know the ways they experience isolation, stigma, humiliation, and other negative aspects of being blind. They get treated like they are young children rather than adults, incapable of doing basic things like going to the bathroom or to keeping a house clean.

To form and build better relationships, arm yourself with knowledge of how you can best help them, and in turn, they will teach you, and have a discussion about how they want you to help them. Do they want your elbow or shoulder to guide them across a dangerous path? Do they want you to tell them where something is on the floor so they can get it themselves or to have you get it for them?

There are potentially dozens, hundreds of people you will meet who have a vision impairment, and you can help make their lives easier just by knowing how to help them. For that to happen, having willingness to learn, patience, understanding, and accepting their refusal of assistance all will contribute to creating a better, more inclusive community for everyone.

When people of the general public understand how to interact with people that are different from themselves, it can propel their relationships, and careers to new heights.

Can You Help Me Now? Series

She will be launching a second book soon called Can You Hear Me Now? A book about how you can interact with people who are Deaf and hard of hearing. The third book, Do You Feel Me Now? will be on how to include the deaf-blind into the community at large. After that will cover many multitudes of disabilities, invisible and not.

About the Author

Tiffany Kohnen can be found on Facebook at www.facebook.com/-DawnOfWriting for all news and books written by her. They include both fiction and non-fiction.

Tiffany grew up in Michigan, so she knows all about the cold! She has Usher Syndrome, a loss of both hearing and sight. Right now, her tunnel vision is at 15% in each eye and wears one cochlear implant in her right ear. She uses oral speech to communicate with people, and knows enough American Sign Language (ASL) to chat with the Deaf.

Growing up, she would waste a ton of paper and stapler, creating books. Much to her teachers, bus drivers, and nanny's' dismay. Tiffany knew she would become an author one day, working on her craft of writing while she read as many books as she could get her hands on. At the same time, she loves to teach people about disabilities, particularly being deaf-blind. Combining her love of writing and educating on disabilities, she found the perfect platform in which to turn her passion into a reality.

Tiffany also loves a lot of other things in life, from doing triathlons to watercolor painting. Most of all, she loves reading and getting into the Word of the Lord. She currently reside in Tampa, FL with her significant other, Richard, and their two crazy daughters and a rescue dog named Buck.

Sources

[1] 40% of visually impaired and blind people are employed at least part-time. This statistics was collected from "Disability Statistics from the 2013 American Community Survey" at Cornell University Employment and Disability Institute. www.disabilitystatistics.org.

[2] 30% of trafficked human beings in Florida has a disability. This statistics was reported at the Family Cafe conference in June 2015, presented by Agency for Persons with Disabilities.